ABIDING

LANDSCAPE OF THE SOUL

*O*ne day of sunshine,
two days of rain.
We stand naked in the forest.

A center so absolutely rich, so
fecund, it appears as nothing;
an emptiness that is fullness, a fullness
that is pure potential — not no-thing, but very
source of every-thing.

Waters of the earth flow to
the sea of that Nothingness as well
as from it; life on this planet being
a most interesting interruption.

Here, I see, is my theory of art. The determination of artistic worth cannot be objective, as in the old days of identifiable cultural authorities and their unambiguous decisions. But neither can it be subjective, as in so much of culture today, leaving all to the feelings and consumer preferences of undeveloped individuals. It must be both objective and subjective, and more. Art must be conversational, meaning that art must move us to give some testimony to that common source which paradoxically finds differentiation uniquely in each one of us. Art needs art to remain art; art needs art to become art. Art both begets and requires what William James described as "the will to believe."

So I am back to my own work, to the miraculous qualities of relationship. It is at this point that I must thank David's agent and my spouse, Diane Rowe of Monroe Fine Art, for introducing me to Lubbers and his luminous photography. My recommendation to the reader is that the relationship with David Lubbers can be fruitful in the most important of human concerns: the seasoning of soul. Dialogue with Lubbers can help us find our way to the origin of our lives. He can help us find the proper meditation or solitude or communing with art or the natural world, returning to our ordinary lives with greater capacity to embody the saving paradox of human existence.

STEPHEN ROWE
Grand Rapids, 1998

INTRODUCTION

David Lubbers's photography has been compelling to me, yet challenging. Virtually all of my work centers on human relation-ship, on the transformation that can occur when we relate to each other in the mode of love and justice. In David's work, though, we rarely see humans, and when they are present, they do not stand out much from the depth of nature.

So why compelling? In viewing David's art, I step back from the "in your face" closeness of media and the so-called direct approach of business and personal life; so many well-maintained faces . . .

Lubbers's art lets us see human presence in a different perspective. He finds and lets pass through his lens a certain latency of the natural world, one that corresponds with our own state of being when we are about to relate out of genuine self. We experience a dis-tinct sense of repose and re-creation (or pre-creation) in viewing David's photos. They help us return to and live from our origin and ground.

Lubbers's photography both reflects and evokes the abode of human life, not as static object, like a building, but rather as dynamic state of being. It is in the state of abiding where I am both most relaxed or receptive and, at the same time, most ready to act. Lubbers' art reminds us of that state of soul from which "the creation of something out of nothing" is possible.

And my verse? It must do more than only explain. In this dialogue with David Lubbers the verse partakes, for better or for worse, in an essential fact of creation: "In the beginning was the word."

By this I mean that just because David's art is so primal, it is vulnerable. It requires interpretation, response, otherwise it could become just pretty pictures, just so much decoration in a culture that cannot tell the difference between art and amusement. Without interpretation of art in relation to nature, the human and the divine, the primal artistic images and immanent spirituality of our era become, as they say in Japan, "painting eyes on chaos."

ABIDING: LANDSCAPE OF THE SOUL

Published 1998 by Wm. B. Eerdmans Publishing Company
255 Jefferson S.E., Grand Rapids, Michigan 49503/
P.O. Box 163, Cambridge CB3 9PU U.K.

Book and cover design: Willem Mineur
Separations: National Correct Color, Grand Rapids, Michigan
Printed in Canada
by Friesens, Altona, Manitoba

02 01 00 99 98   5 4 3 2 1

Library of Congress Cataloging-in-Publication Data

Lubbers, David, 1947–
Abiding: landscape of the soul / David Lubbers and Stephen Rowe.
p.   cm.
ISBN 0-8028-3859-6   (hardcover: alk. paper)
1. Landscape photography—United States.   2. Lubbers, David, 1947–
I. Rowe, Stephen C., 1945–   . II. Title.
TR660.5.L83   1998
779'.3673–dc21   98-34647
CIP

Abiding

LANDSCAPE OF THE SOUL

David Lubbers and Stephen Rowe

WILLIAM B. EERDMANS PUBLISHING COMPANY

GRAND RAPIDS, MICHIGAN / CAMBRIDGE, U.K.

"That the world is, is the mystical,"
that rock out of which flows
the purest water of truth.

4

*G*od meets us at the
rock, the altar, the stairs.

God meets God on the shore
and in the desert.

We meet God in the eyes of the other.

aring goodness, love that is
all around;
daring the gift quality of life,
the openness of this freedom
rather than the illusion security
of our failure, warfare, demise.

We cannot save ourselves, but apparently
we are capable of refusal and ruin.

*D*ecentered in space,
loose, barely embodied, streaming vapors all over.

Descent to Earth involves concentration, a coming
to mass and density, the incarnation. Resistance of
atmosphere causes friction to burn off strands of
dread and refusal, ribboning out behind us in flame.
Cleansing occurs as we come to Earth,
taking full body.

. . . continuing
after birth, through physical and emotional maturity,
spiritual emptying. In fact, the process may not be
complete until our bodies give out
and we are ready to leave. It may even take
several lifetimes for the work of this planet
to be finished with us.

*N*ight so completely serene,
all clouds
slip down
from dome of sky,
to the edge
all around.

12

13

ight, air,
Nothingness,
ruins

14

*T*he great teachings allow us
to be accepted
in the power and the safety
of our vulnerability.

Clear, cool finally penetrates
    stormy heat,
    breaking up clouds, dispersing,
    blowing them on down over the horizon:

once more the event of creation.

*T*rees and walls and
rocks and people (some in heaven,
some in hell, some waiting).
Water
Flesh
Clouds.
How utterly astonishing
our instant here (a time scented
with dim remembering).

Along with inability to see lakes and forests, so much of our psychological way fails to see the human being too. It sees parts, problems, functions, but so rarely the whole. And humans, like lakes and forests, unlike machines, will not be treated this way. More even than complex and mysterious ecosystems, humans can only be treated as wholes with parts (never as just parts that happen to hang or crank together), or either rebellion or submission will follow and humanity will simply disappear.

*R*ocks still, rocks moving,
rocks a waterfall,
then an altar.

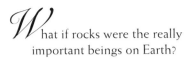

What if rocks were the really
important beings on Earth?

24

To treat the self as one,
but not more than one. This
is to be awake

id God create everything, the one and
the many, from His/Her act?
Or did it All, God too if you will,
just flow from . . . ?
And if God, then who is that other
voice telling the story ("In the
beginning, God created . . .")?
For that matter, what is the universe doing
now through you and me asking the question?

*W*e speak, relate, are
present. And we are silent.
Each of these must be complete.
In the middle our problems lie;
in full simultaneity we live
the radiant paradox
of our salvation.

Problems are never gone. They perpetuate.
We cannot deny them, must even
befriend them if we can.
But to dwell upon them, to sink
into them,
to coddle them, is surely one of the more perverse
indulgences of this modern freedom.

*T*he ice takes forever to melt.
It melts.
As does the stone.

$\mathcal{W}$here do we come from?
  — what dimension, imagination, soup.
Where will we go? — to heaven, or dust,
or future worlds?
What am I doing here,
and why is it so hard for me to be present?

*W*hen I first came to this planet
I was enshrouded in ego, clouded by emotion.
Now I see more clearly.

31

*M*any ancestors
taught disdain for the Earth.
Now Earth responds
with a challenge: to accept
the gift of life,
including our own. Can we love
what is here on this well-worn
planet?

A car comes to the place
where the rocks talk
in shadow language to one another.

The car stays for only a phrase or two,
then returns to the Earth.

Without mother rock
we are weathervanes in foul air:
twirl, stop,
point one way then another,
back, stop, quiver, point again.
Of course, without father sky
we die of the ordinary
becalmed —
where gravity
is about the only thing happening.

36

*T*his planet is
not yet finished.
To help, we contain
within ourselves the anguish of separation,
and the unremitting sorrow of death.
— and we live with
what zest we can.

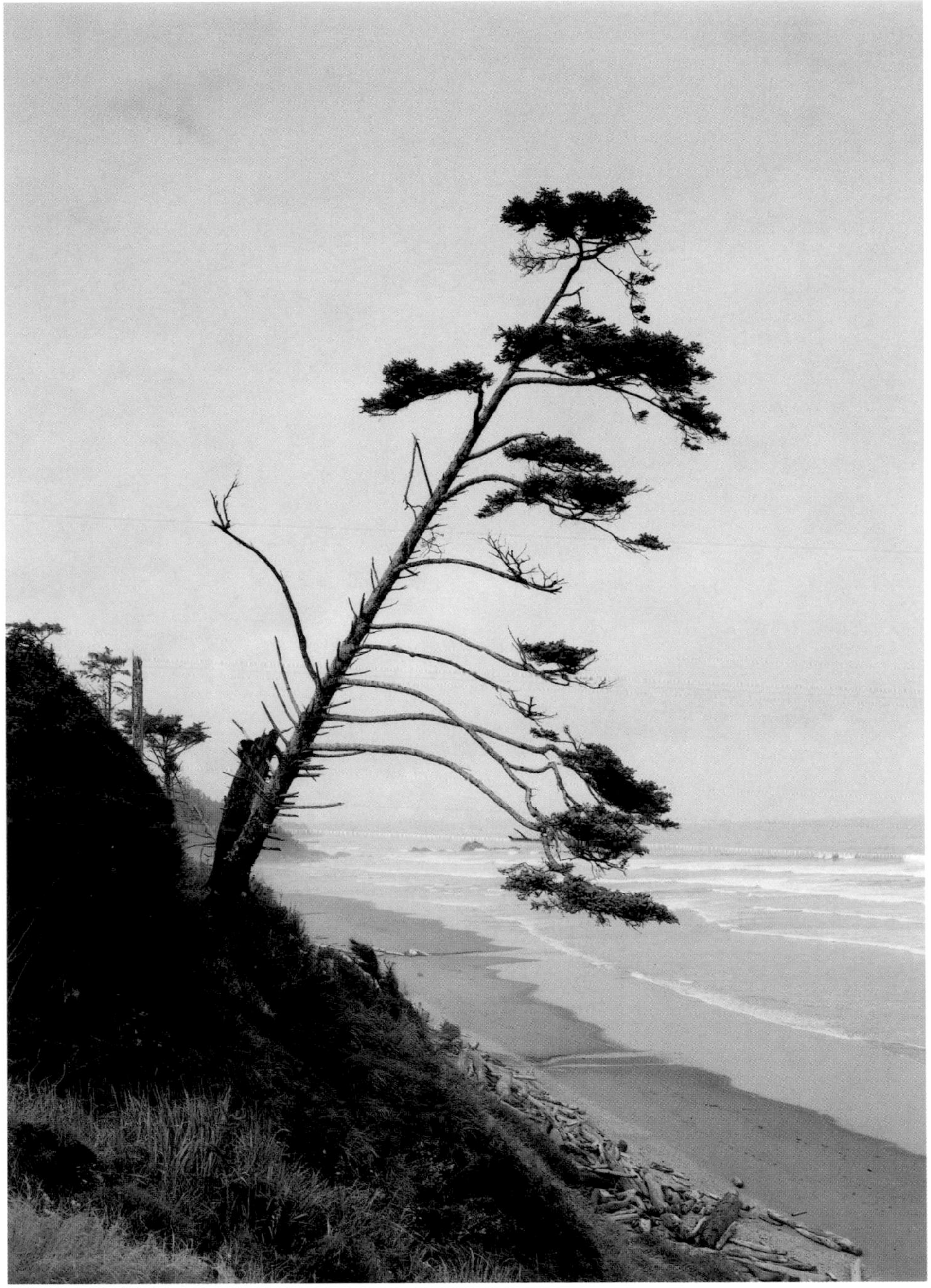

People give up — on love and
relationship, enchantment, God,
possibility, hope.
They crouch within themselves,

close in upon themselves,
supposing in protection, while turning
from what they have sadly concluded
to be absent.

*W*e fly, we do—
   perhaps in the night while sleeping,
   or in split instants when eyes blink, yet
   also actually in the light of day in planes:
   from cloudcover complete, grey enveloping,
   through flickering light — dark, light, see
   something, see nothing — then into sunshine.
   When we are fortunate we cruise the clear,
   calm air, though most life does flicker.

*D*o not let anyone lure you
or frighten you out of that
calm place within yourself
where God reposes, for that
is your home and your temple,
your refuge and your adventure.

*W*e are beings incarnate
and incarnating, bodied and embodying.
Do we embody our fear, or is it love
that finds body through us?

*W*inter light,
champagne,
slanted, oblique;
more precious for its remoteness,
and the improbability of its promise.

*L*et me live my wisdom,
what my soul knows and loves and yearns for —
but has not yet been able to body.
I can do it with you, not without you, your
trust, your definiteness, the possibilities
of your planet.

Perhaps this is the prayer of creation.

*E*arth would perhaps not need us,
except how would she look upon
her glory? As hawks and wolves,
fish do? Yet would she feel
the thrill and pathos
of being?

That God is love;
that God somehow enters and moves in the world
through the eyes and the acts
of human beings —
this is why we sing of the dignity of all people.

*S*tairs silent,
leading ghostly figures both ways.

*L*ife dies,
life is reborn;
   life acts, life accepts; we all submit.

   Yesterday I was afraid,
   depressed.
   today I am reborn, steady,
   containing yesterday's wish for deliverance
   at the same time I am exuberant.

   To catch the rhythm of this — not
   wallowing or being lost in the death times,
   not failing to act; yet not short-circuiting,
   drugging, fleeing them, or
   paying their ransom.

   Here grace is infused, between
   self and self, convening the space of the
   relationship in which each
   can laugh with the other,
   and the self can be whole,
   two in one, one in two.

A tuned human being
is most magnificent.
When those energies that otherwise swirl and conflict,
pull against each other, leak out or fly off —
when these energies are in concentrated, harmonious order,
in relation, in a life well-lived,
here is the glory of God.
Here is presence.

$\mathcal{E}$vil in this time (perhaps all
time) is the confounding of hope
and promise, communion of any kind,
closing the horizon of possibility, denying
anything higher than disappointment's raging
against those
whose faith alone keeps
the light of fulfillment from going out.

True seeing and right intuition,
or a projection from our own
pain?
How are we to know the difference
between the two?

Earth is heaven,
though humans see it as bad
at first, because
we project false-self-pain
upon the planet, all over.

Humans here release
our fear-ignorance-desire,
our clinging to the false. Once we let go
of our unhappiness, we can be in heaven
for the time remaining.

INDEX OF PHOTOGRAPH TITLES

58

INDEX OF PHOTOGRAPH TITLES